Disinformation

FRANCES LEVISTON was born in Edinburgh in 1982. She grew up in Sheffield and read English at St Hilda's College, Oxford. In 2006 she received an Eric Gregory Award from the Society of Authors. *Public Dream*, her first collection, was published in 2007 by Picador and shortlisted for the T. S. Eliot Prize, the Forward Prize for Best First Collection and the Jerwood-Aldeburgh First Collection Prize. Her poems have appeared in *Poetry*, the *London Review of Books*, the *Guardian*, *The Times*, the *TLS*, and various anthologies.

Also by Frances Leviston

Public Dream

Frances Leviston

Disinformation

PICADOR

First published 2015 by Picador
an imprint of Pan Macmillan, a division of Macmillan Publishers Limited
Pan Macmillan, 20 New Wharf Road, London N1 9RR
Basingstoke and Oxford
Associated companies throughout the world
www.panmacmillan.com

ISBN 978-1-4472-7114-7

George Seferis. *George Seferis: Collected Poems*.
Translated and edited by Edmund Keeley and Phillip Sherrard.
© 1995 Princeton University Press.
Reprinted by permission of Princeton University Press.

1 3 5 7 9 8 6 4 2

A CIP catalogue record for this book is available from the British Library.

Printed and bound by CPI Group (UK) Ltd, Croydon, CR0 4YY

Contents

I

Disinformation 3

GPS 5

Pyramid 6

Bishop in Louisiana 8

The Bridge in the Mirror 10

A Token 11

IUD 13

Iresine 14

Parma Violet 15

The Paperweight 16

II

The Golden Age 21

Sulis 22

Woodland Burial 28

Hill Top Fort 29

Emblem 30

Propylaea 31

Reconstruction 34

Attica 36

Midsummer Loop 38

Athenaeum 40

III

The Taiga 49

Kassandra 50

Trimmings 53

Caribou 56

Octagonal Rug 58

The Eclipse 59

Memory Foam 61

The Historical Voice 64

A Shrunken Head 65

Story 69

Acknowledgements 71

I woke with this marble head in my hands;
it exhausts my elbows and I don't know where to put it down.
It was falling into the dream as I was coming out of the dream
so our life became one and it will be very difficult for it to separate again.

George Seferis, 'Mythistorema'
Trans. Edmund Keeley and Philip Sherrard

Lying is done with words, and also with silence.

Adrienne Rich, 'Women and Honor: Some Notes on Lying'

I

Disinformation

I am making jelly
for my nephew's fourth birthday party,
any flavour as long as it's red,
bouncy cubes snipped and stirred into hot water
in a cloudy Pyrex dish,
rediscovering the secret of isinglass,
or is it horse gelatin, while a radio announcer
intimates that certain unpopular
facts about the operations
hitherto repressed, like signs removed
from crossroads and bridges in occupied lands,
can now be revealed, if we just stay tuned.

Party bags designed
to please infants pile on the counter,
too-bright colours, badly made; blue napkins,
party-poppers; my red hands
put cylinders of sausage on cocktail sticks
(these pass for traditions)
and all the time I listen to them talk
fluently about foreknowledge, proactivity, stations.
It is winter,
treacherous to walk.
The children are on their way by now,
adults too, bundled against the promise of snow

and the entertainer, with tricks and jokes
hidden under a blanket in the boot of his Volvo,
limp balloons into which he will blow
his lungs full of ideal animals, practises misdirection.
I chop yellow cheese. Out the kitchen window
the whirligig turns, metal spokes
merciless as diagrams
cutting the air
no clothing softens, tiny gems
icing the nodes where their lines intersect.
Every extant leaf is fixed
with glitter where the glue's dried clear.

GPS

Like a wet dream this snow-globe was a gift
to myself. She rides shotgun

or stuck to the dashboard, swirling and swirling
across the carpet of potholes to my house.

Mantelpiece matryoshka,
she wears an inscrutable face:

there's no telling how many dolls deep she goes
beyond her one red peanut-shell,

her pupa's lacquered shine,
superglued to a painted knoll, brilliantly magnified

by an atmosphere of cerebrospinal fluid
under the smooth glass dome's museum,

a solid case of ozone.
When I do a U-turn it triggers another storm.

Her compass boggles. Lie down there in that drift,
little girl, you're feeling strangely warm,

and something big is about to make sense
if we just keep going in the opposite direction.

Pyramid

All along the skyline, cranes
quiet above rooftops,
conspicuous as knives dropped
vertically into carpet,

folded ironing-board-upright
or set at right-
angles, corner brackets
bolting the sky to the ground.

They dangle claws on chains,
unbaited hooks
balanced by elevated breeze-blocks,
into the unfinished town,

fishing a pond
that hasn't been stocked.
Their paintwork's bright as macs
in rain, or the mops and pans

a woman once persuaded me to sell
door to door,
describing in the air
of her living room a pyramid,

most mysterious
of all mysterious extancies, her red
nail climbing floors
to the vertex, where it stood

or floated
as she effortlessly said
*In no time at all
you'll have a lifestyle just like mine.*

Through the cranes'
necks the cloud-burst rings,
across the clad-
stone hotel still missing

its penthouse, its punchline,
bucketing down
like the old cartoon
where a skeleton drinks champagne.

Bishop in Louisiana

Twelve days since I took up my post in this village,
a handful of clapboard houses crowded round the harbour
and the concrete yards glittering with scales
where church groups serve up grits and tamales
from long trestle tables and the interiors of white vans.

I myself eat at the hotel: beef, pasta, anything but fish,
watching the black sea break foamlessly
against the chemical barricade. On its surface orange curds
ride like surfboards or children's life-preservers.
After dinner I take my coffee in the privacy of my suite.

There is little to accomplish here. I walk on the beach
where the nests of common terns driven upwind to breed
are marked with red flags mounted on popsicle sticks,
hundreds of them, bunting in the wind. Each nest is no more
than a dint in the sand, easily made with a fist.

Yesterday I saw a dead sea-turtle turning to soup
inside its own shell. I am not immune to the irony of this.
I write cheques for the fishermen fitting their boats
with booms to skim the water, and speak to sad newscasters
under a flypast of helicopters and a crop-duster salute.

Try to imagine what a hundred million litres means.
You can't. At night, before bed, in the surprisingly deep bath,
I push my big toe into the streaming faucet
and feel its pressure turn to a hot, relentless gush,
nightmarishly pleasurable, like pissing myself in my sleep.

The Bridge in the Mirror

Power flares on command from a central faucet
into the white tub of the flagship hotel,
confirming our worst suspicions of comfort,
whipping the clear worm of complimentary gel
to a fairies' castle, unsupportable. Testimony
built round air-conditioned air and a dose of sparkle
dissolves when a live somebody enters
with their oils and smells that melon-tinted water.

The summit is over. Protesters disperse
against plastic shield-walls tough as double-glazing.
Orderly behind panelled veneer, the mini-bar
committee sits in darkness for the hour
it's called upon, no expenses spared, cutesy bottles
rattling in their seats when the choppers pass,
like draft dodgers jumpy in the House of Representatives,
like working class heroes in the House of Lords.

Arms and legs exiting through the bathwater's lens
to reliable applause from extractor fans
bend at strange angles, without broken bones, revealing
a second, smaller person, peacefully submerged
and dormant as a property that no one seems to own.
The midget hairdryer and the bible abridged
in the mirror belong to her. That foot would fit the shoe
in the heritage museum two clicks from here.

A Token

In the poky attic
bedroom a bit-broken
cocktail umbrella
made of blonde toothpicks
and crêpe paper
printed with bamboo
stands proud of a shut
paperback book

on the tallest shelf –
a shiny edition
of *Hamlet* or *Othello*,
incidental not symbolic –
downcasting its tiny
disc of shade
under the damp skylight.
You'd miss it at first

then find it garish,
a finch in the Dolomites
glued to a tree,
trembling in the noonday
blaze to be found
by the bird-catcher,
seized-upon,
pickled and crunched.

Somebody sentimental
kept it
close after dinner
in a Japanese restaurant
decorated just
like a joke about Japan –
waitress in kimono,
walls hung with ideograms,

an indoor pool
where fat gold carp
drift under a wooden bridge,
drifted, never swam . . .
Well, but what
is sentiment? Emotion
out of time
with its occasion?

Pocketed, then
with a flourish produced
right in the middle
of an argument, there it stands:
a wish-coin welded
to the tiles of a fountain,
a green anachronistic
needle in the head.

IUD

This gadget intrudes so nothing else can. It froths
the way a widget froths beer, agitant,

dispenses with the problem of abstinence — *don't* —
and plants a dull pea under the mattress.

Childless. Sleepless. Rings on cushions do this too,
diamonds in the toilet. *I placed a jar in Tennessee;*

in the wilderness I buried my witch's bottle,
half-full of screws, pins, piss and curse blood,

keeping a promise in a place I've forgotten.
A prize in every box! A mine in a mitten. Automated

night-time sprinkler system. The walk-in wardrobe's
coat-hangers cannon and tinkle, turning to hooks.

Iresine

Shocking pink and plasticky-looking,
like something that would titivate an antechamber
or teach medics nerves,
its leaves contuse around their perimeters.

When the sunset shines through it, it responds in kind,
glowing until the horizon intervenes
as if it doesn't belong on land.

Picture it undersea, thriving on saline,
whining theremin-ethereal where the underwaves
wash through its rounded dividends, its tender branches
impersonating anemone and coral,

parts forever colourful
and moist and scared: flinching clitoral architecture,
the glans inside its cowl.

Parma Violet

Egyptian sofas, old anaglypta,
the drop-leaf table where the pine tree posed
every mild December,
on its pedestal the dodo, crackle-glazed,
and hung above the hearth and the dormant fire
a painting I supposed

must be a distant cousin, or a great grandmother,
but was neither of those —
only a junk-shop likeness of a stranger,
all tarnished oils and shadows,
that when my friends visited made them shudder
in the cruel, exaggerated manner of girls.

A Gothic effect, the narrow shoulder
turned aside, the plain, black, high-necked blouse;
governess, or dowager,
she looked severe to them. I found her serious,
and since there was no other
for her I invented any history that pleased:

hair powder, mystic wills, Parma
violets dry on the tongue, big lozenges loose
in iconic tins, and the sampler's
motto: *Family is Furniture* — charge to which I rose
in spite of myself, like a hair in thunder —
if I wasn't hers, then whose?

The Paperweight

From Chambord-pink at the base, it clears
to where the upper curve reflects
a skull-cap of charcoal, giving the Earth's atmosphere
in miniature: the sea, the air, then space.
Erupting from that wavy cocktail is a white flower
like a frozen whale-spout arrested mid-expulsion,
a filigree fuchsia trumpet, petals
peeling in a spray, bearing among them a bubble
shaped like a long inverted tear-drop, an airy utterance
trapped in the glass.

There's no remembering now where it came from,
gift with no giver, a solid glass fruit
more ovoid than round, more plum than orange,
a novelty not for consumption
weighing as much as a pint of milk
compressed in the palm, all fingers braced to hold it
as it slows the hand
better than the papers for which it's designed,
one end levelled off so it can stand
steady on my desk and keep my desk on the ground.

At eye level, gazing through its distances, I see
tall violet chrysanthemum gates
opening through interstellar emptiness
on boiling horizons, and a huge hand grasping
at the jewelled arrangement, five smudged knuckles
on which the weight sits like the purple stone
caught in brass claws on my mother's cocktail ring,
too vivid, never worn, stuck in the dark
of its velvet box, over which I and my brother fought
bitterly, wanting her to will it to us.

I touch the weight to my forehead. Cold
safety glass in the car's back seat:
coming home from a stay with family friends,
the arm-rest's velveteen sofa down
and my forearms raked with effervescent pink
scores left by cats' claws when cats don't want picking up,
I saw petrol refineries ranged along the firth
at sunset puff their blinds of cloud
across a rosy sky doubled in the running
waters few salmon survive.

Knowing where one noxious cloud began
and the next faded was hard, I would say distressing;
likewise determining where pink turned grey
or vice versa made me carsick. It was the apprehension
of a difference also seamless,
too fine for the fingertips, like a sentence
you seem to have understood but can't make sense of,
or something being done for you
without your permission, under the flag of helpfulness,
to which you can raise no legitimate objection.

I lift it higher, the weight, in my hand,
opening the iron gates of the zoo
where a pair of brass falcons in fretwork hoops
roost forever, and someone in summer
pointed out hippos half-sunk in muddy pools, sealed
as neoprene-impregnable as olives, all grey and rounded,
until they yawned and their muzzles unfolded
bluntly, padded, gammon-pink,
showing teeth as long and smooth as tent-pegs
hammered into the gums.

II

The Golden Age

In the golden age, we communed with gods.
A god could be hidden, barely contained,
inside the costumes of normal men.
Nothing was certain. How could you refuse
a beggar's request or a gambler's wager,
the bold advance of the boss's only daughter,
without fear of causing offence to a god?
You would say yes. In the golden age,
whatever was offered, you would say yes.

Sulis

1.

When Sulis rose from the open ground
and entered Minerva, she mastered that shape
with such perfection she seemed to vanish
under history's golden heel,

as if Minerva sank one foot in the fountain
and poured her rival off –
only to hear in her victory-moment
a worshipper offer verbatim the prayer

Sulis drew from his mouth before,
as lovers change loved ones more than words;
only to find her eyes in the mirror
swam with someone else's tears.

2.

The gap between Senuna's teeth,
which took a thick coin or the edge of a sword,
the slit between worlds, a problem
and a wish, gushed with water day and night

into the trampled midden she ruled:
Sulis's mother, her predecessor,
recipient of plaques and the clasps of hoods,
songs and bones, the model of a lion,

who vanished after Sulis did.
There are several ways of dissolving:
to soak yourself in the baths is one;
to let the muds meet above your head is another.

3.

That owl gone hunting is the ghost
of Desdemona, or at least her after-image:
corneas domed, a dropped-hanky
breast in the dark. Sulis would love her

credulous glare, the warm
mouse making its way down her gullet,
surrendering fur and ears and claws
the better to join her entourage,

and the story of how she started flying
her own feather bolster and long white ribbon,
displaced from the palace
not by a mistress, but by an avatar.

4.

Pellets indistinguishable from seed-husks
tighten round an emptiness.
Hands without another hand to hold make fists.
Under the willows

discarded vessels, void of fluid,
ache for Sulis to love them again, not leave them
there in the succulent grass.
Already she is forgetting their faces;

she leans to spit in her lover's mouth
and makes a bridge, a casual suspension
involving them both,
like spider-silk draped from cactus to cactus.

5.

Here they are, Pallas, Minerva,
with hair so heavy it bows their heads
and grey thick ankles they cool where the river
slows its rush in a kind of pond.

Nothing beyond their bodies concerns them,
nothing beyond the pools of light
their own lamps throw.
They did what they could in their time, and now

the boys who briefly rest in their shadows
cannot matter much to them,
as much as the veiled
flies on cows' faces bother the cows.

6.

Water's not particular, but where it passes is;
water like wisdom resists capture,
never complacent, revising itself
according to each new container it closes.

The heart thrives on syncresis. Sulis
hearts each man she kisses,
each costume she wears, each nakedness.
Like formal dresses,

she carries them with her into the cloud,
its floating parade
of people who laundered her difficult feelings
until she put them aside.

Woodland Burial

Thrown water touched him and where it touched it said
his body was the same brownness leaves turn
when autumn is upon us, a swept-up heap
trembling where it stood,
that when the huntress concentrated
trees, tree-shadows, underbrush and bushes made a wood
and it was ever thus, that nothing can be other than as known
by a god, no truth a lie, no death long sleep.

Poised with springy longbow drawn
and back to the sun, the one who had revealed her form
from landscape or eyes
independent as a streak of white paint on a mirror
held him on her gaze
and held the torn canopy of clouds on the water
as she might have kept a spoonful of honey in the warm
fold of her tongue before it dissipated.

Not the greatest possible harm,
which needs to be known and named as such
to achieve its end, not what he fled, but the unofficial crime,
the moment she let her attention crop
those deep recursive avenues of beech to a backdrop
he broke against, confused,
so nothing in the landscape escaped his touch
and nothing left of him was in the picture she composed.

Hill Top Fort

Up here, the highest
vantage point for miles, the walls' red
stones find a counterpart for their silence
in the clouds, the closest of which reveal themselves
by seeming to pass much faster
than the rest from this

comparatively
low perspective. Their long shadows
outrace us underfoot like thoughts. Sea-salt
castigates the wind and whitens the vertical
acre of scrub down to the shore,
or sharpens up the

disembodied cries
of cold birds. Almost unnoticed,
all around, the carnelian ants work,
oblivious to their *pleasant seat*, whose boot they
circumnavigate or vanish
underneath. For an

hour, what some men take
upon themselves can seem, if not
forgivable, familiar at least:
how distance makes immensities manoeuvrable,
toy blocks of shipping containers
tumbled on the docks.

Emblem

A honeybee pinned to my thumb!
Its legs close, instantly done,
the claws of a setting shutting round a stone,
a rampant lion
brandishing its motto in manly arms.
O memory of form,
spending your sting in defence of the realm,
what medals you've become!

Propylaea

It is properly
the gate before the gate,
the entrance before the entrance,
a huge tautology

made of marble
and the old ambition
to be understood in a certain way.
The long approach

up hairpin
rubble resembling steps
towards the massive entablature
and baking summit

frames blue sky
and the heads of those
who comprehend in the foreground;
it glorifies

more than ever
the sanctuaries waiting
beyond, behind these colonnades'
unprotected sides.

When there is
an opening but no dividing
wall, the emphasis falls on process
instead of destination –

that is to say,
you come with your hands
shielding your eyes, in deference,
or not at all;

and those of us
who make the passage
correctly cannot return by the same
route that shut

its eye invisibly
after we entered and hope
for the change to happen in reverse:
we are stuck

in the kingdom
of knowledge we came
here for, too perfectly primed
inductees of a cult

finding what
they thought was true
more true when it finally occurs,
forms emerging

as the dust clears,
enormous structures
maintaining their perspectives
from the deep past

to here. It has
all been done before:
original figures, the seven plots.
We can relax

beside the stone-
sandaled caryatids,
their unmoved skirts giving shade
from the sun

as it's shone
for millions of years,
lighting all this toil and splendour;
can feel our own

ambitions recede
then colossally resurge,
partial and imposing like the gate
before the gate,

hinged on nothing,
promising this: *if there is
an opening but no dividing wall,
the emphasis falls* . . .

Reconstruction

after 'The Ruin'

The future creates these fabulous blueprints
from cities it pulls to the ground. What seems the work of giants
lies diminished: domes cave, towers like telescopes
collapse upon themselves, the icy gate
like a berg breaks up, and hoar-frost serves as poor man's grout.
All promises of sanctuary disband into dust
as the centuries pass. The earth's fist
closes on the architects, cold and catacombed,
while a hundred generations live above their heads.

Here, for example: here stood a wall,
bearded with lichen and swabbed with blood, not swayed by storms
or the rise and fall of kingdom after kingdom.
Tall or deep, it tumbled at last;
only thrown stones remain, moulded by the wind,
going on milling against themselves
down in the grass. Where once the light of knowledge lay
across these fiddly crafts, mud-crusts offer up
proof of a mind that quickly wove
its ringed design, and that someone sharp
bound the wall-braces together with wire.

Think how intricate the city must have been: archipelagos
of bathing-pools, bristling gables, the bored glint of swords on patrol,
and open casks at every corner
round which camaraderie spiralled like confetti
orbiting a plug-hole –
until the future finished all that.

Bodies piled three men deep for miles. A city of bones
it must have been, and what disease bred
in that grand decomposition claimed the remaining artisans.
Time turned their temples into desecrated tombs.
The whole endeavour came undone. Idols of clay and the talented hands
that shaped them lay in bare scratched graves. Fences flattened.
This red curved ceremonial roof
drops its tiles from the ceiling-vault: civilization
falls to the floor in dribbling heaps

like everything else, here, where many a man of the past,
blazing with wine, blinding in the spoils of war,
bounced his gaze from treasure to treasure, gold to silver, coins to trinkets,
rings to cups, pinballing angles round the faceted rock
of the mirrored enclosure's endless reign,
here, where stone buildings stood, flowing water threw out heat
in massive clouds, and the mortar circled
the known world within its embrace, where the baths lay, hot as hearts
that prize their own convenience.

Attica

We have noticed the house at the end's
original golden shell of smoke-discoloured stones
being elaborated upon —
then the funds, the pretence of funds, ran dry.

New cement buttercreams the breeze-blocks together.
The tough blue tub it was mixed inside
matures to found sculpture, a reverse mould for rainfall
on permanent display in the yard;

those grey runny hollows, like pinnacles of guano
at a cliff's foot, if cast would turn out an architect's model
so spectacular, so irregular,
no one could think it possible to execute.

Seven flexible silvery extractor tubes flop
from the chimney stack,
the arms of a villain in *Doctor Who*, never as new
as you wish it would be, a riff on a form;

and finial tiles, faintly martial,
decorate the ridge with a crest of spikes, four-pointed stars
touching tip to tip, a string of paper dolls
holding hands forever, all cut from the same sheet

by someone who also peels oranges in one go.
Terracotta warriors, Tanagra figurines,
their *fin de siècle* welcoming party interrupts the sky
with its colour-wheel opponent, orange on blue,

and a gallon jug of paint stripper, colourless and violent,
stands forgotten on the tar paper roof.
It must be a reminder someone left for themselves
of something they meant to do.

Midsummer Loop

now in the stillness, the two still hours
between this meeting and that,
hours of silence in which the angel of conversation deserts us
to beat her wings above another gathering,
another long room, magnificent table and solemn pronouncement
made to the detriment of everybody else
and the glorification of the subject,
now we are abandoned to our own resources
on this one original summer's day
and two hours fill like stones with the heat of the afternoon,
two flat stones placed on the stomach to steady
the heartbeat and the breathing,
a number of rabbits
emerge from their secret holes hidden about campus,
hidden but not undiscoverable holes
down in the beginnings of dry holly-bushes out of season
and the naked wooden roots of rhododendrons
from which the rabbits hop forward one hop at a time, one a minute,
a hundred little clepsydras
all set to different schedules, forward
on to the grass, where they balance, weightless as empty pelts
on the points of the blades, like martial artists
who lie unharmed on beds of nails
conducting their spiritual business, with two hot stones
weighing down their bodies, lightly, painlessly,
rabbits fanning out
across the sweeps of grass that sustain them,

across the blades that do not bend beneath them,
where they eat with endless hunger and fanatical devotion,
clipping flat the sharp tips
precisely with ordinary, curved, discoloured teeth
again and again, masticating the strands
as they cross and re-cross the blocks of dark gold sun
laid across the lawns like golden doors
through which we cannot pass, through which they pass unharmed,
both ears laid flat like banked canoes
and their great hind legs gentle and relaxed,
white scuts bobbing
quietly across the campus, which is also their campus,
attached as rabbits are attached to their shadows
to a vast university invisible underground, the one ours mirrors,
intricate halls of residence and studios
round which the rabbits conduct themselves
in absolute darkness, by touch and smell alone, the wordless
sensitivities of their whiskers
brushing the walls and other warm bodies
or thrilling to an offensive discharge of fear in the air
undetectable to the human
who feels so pleased to have spotted
two rabbit-holes, there, at the foot of that blossoming tree,
now in the stillness, the two still hours
between this meeting and that

Athenaeum

1.

Your bond has matured! Time to collect:
time to biopsy the ingrown boil
you've brought to term on your forehead.
So Zeus bore the staggering

migraine of Athena
like an antler incipient on his parting
until the burden proved
too much, the brain-child challenged

too closely the brain, and blunt Hephaestus
chopped her out.
Let's see what, if anything, you've managed
in the way of inner resources.

2.

Club of one, memory palace,
where membership *per annum* costs
the time it takes to visit,
climb there now in the culminating light

of a brimstone sunset
against which the intimated mountains
firm their peaks; climb there now
and claim what's yours,

your abrogate inheritance.
Bring your own wire
if you want the place fencing:
bring your own game if you want it stocked.

3.

This is the home of compulsive hoarders,
as packed to the roof with fire-risks
as lungs with alveola.
It wheezes and expands, a concertina,

no pipes just valves, all wallpaper and no walls,
inscribable surfaces laid face to face,
economies of area
fusing and fanning like blinds in a storm

that blatter the light
and vivisect long views with kaleidoscopic
panic – one turn too many
or one too few.

4.

Heroic moths labour
round the lighting-rig at the open-air
amphitheatre;
heathenish and stately, semicircular

marble benches give off a moony glow,
as if the imaginable might
still happen: dead leaves and dumb signage
clear the sunken stage

for threnodies and lectures;
or a tourist decide
not to steal rocks from the unprotected
structure, though he could.

5.

If you fall asleep in a temple, be prepared
to wake with your ear licked clean as a conch
and the statements of the gods
suddenly cold and clear to you, suddenly a cinch,

even as the speech of those you loved
loses all succulence
and withers on the branch. To drift so exposed
in an icon's presence

among the burnt offerings, the wine left to breathe,
is to give your compliance.
The dead lie still in dictatorships of silence:
nothing says nothing in their sinuses and mouths.

6.

Minerva born of Jupiter,
out of the undamageable godhead drawn,
guard our sororities that know
no better; shed blessings as we pass

gossiping through the metal-detector doors
on campus, pillars of books
from reading lists
piled against our chests; shield the past

as under a hood of Victorian stone
your own shrine rests,
all but turned to a palimpsest,
in Edgar's Field, in Handbridge, in Chester.

III

The Taiga

Cold crown of the world. Boreas exhales
the breath that's preserved him all these years,
kept the wolverine alive, and the spruce-blue stars
keen as crystals of virgin ice
clipping the pines on their northern slopes.

Most coverage here is evergreen.
It grows in the short day painfully slow,
putting down rings, and whatever waxed needles do
pitter to the ground
lie there still as pick-up-sticks in the reckoning

between two goes, as if the soft lynx
left these miles on long exposure. Bison graze,
moss-obsessed. Fresh snow settling confuses them
with abandoned dens and boulders.
A she-bear, snug in the bed of her own fur,

lies under stone, four pink cubs
assuming their forms faster in her womb
than the carcasses that nourished them can decompose.
She dreams at double speed
of balsam wood, hot piss and foreign males,

the planet turning imperceptibly
underneath her shoulder. Honey congeals
in hives suspended from conifer boughs. The yellow
eyes of a Tengmalm's owl
click in the dark like camera shutters.

Kassandra

We touch down in Siviri, on Kassandra,
the first spiral arm. A mantis dries in the myrtle.
Moths drag their abdomens through the fluid sand
in eternity symbols. The sea, antagonized
a cloudy blue, banks long drifts
of ticker-tape seaweed up against the pilings.
The air smells of salt, and the sweetness of pines
that weep thin syrup to the compound earth,
their long, pliable, pale green needles
managing to droop and spike at the same time.

White skies overcast, and calm, and close.
The beach loses contrast like a film too long exposed:
nacre-coloured, ivory, silver, shell.
The lukewarm water doesn't wave, it breathes.
I lie flat on a flat cool dune,
my cardigan for a pillow, ear-down. The raised
spine of my book makes a rampart
where a tiny brown spider sits, proprietorially
taking the view. Sometimes he puts
his four front legs in the air and feels around,
checking the humidity, or hailing a friend.
When the sun touches him he shines like resin,
half-transparent. His face is a shield,
almost the size of the hooded crows' hoods
of beaten mail, where they mooch beyond him,
then jump into the air like they're jumping on to the ground.

Further down the beach, teenage boys
are dismantling a tiki bar's wooden umbrellas.
They dig long palings out of the sand,
kept damp all season where they sharpen
to pencil-points at the ends, and rest them on their sides.
The shades, made of matted old tinder,
tile in overlapping panels towards us –
a solar field or a shield-wall at distance, the scales
of a lizard seen up close. Then the boys
carry them into the gloomy bar-room, in columns,
lightly as leafcutter ants delivering
doilies of privet to their underground posts.

Eagerly the restaurateur by the taxi rank
welcomes us, his only patrons, to a blue-painted table
and disposable white paper table-cloth.
Stray cats leap and drop into the garbage dumpers.
Across the gulf we can see Mount Olympus
melt the red sun like a bath-pearl on its peak.
The Russian girl who serves us is blonde and sad,
her eyes, born too far apart,
watery and pale as peeled cucumber. She wants to talk.
The chickpea soup and the octopus are good.
Her best friend married an Englishman
and moved away last year. There was a terrible fire here
that burnt the whole village down to the stone.
Everybody saw it happen on the news.
Things haven't been the same. She sounds like someone
from another time, someone with an open wound.

Ouzo turns white when it touches ice,
like people's eyes in the presence of angels.
The cubes revolve in its milky emulsion.
Tomorrow the sea will be plaster and the sky plaster-cast.
Already three cafés and the patîsserie are closed.
An old man sits at the end of the quay,
watching the caïques darken through his cataracts.
He catches fish too small to eat.
The rollers turn white when they hit the rocks.

Trimmings

1. *Frangelico*

It slops from coppery
    glass Dominican cassocks
thicker than water,
    thinned syrup crackling
and smoking over ice,
    pale as hearts of hazelnuts
half-caramelized
    or relics lit in cabinets.
Angelic alcoholic for kids,
    all quickening sweetness
without the burnt palate,
    it's praline, gilt, milk chocolate.
Don't knock it. Also,
    don't drink a lot of it.
Handy mnemonic for nuts
    and Alps, the Piedmont
and Languedoc, *Our Father*,
    fluent Occitan, Orthodox
baroque brass fixtures,
    all the schmaltzy
terror of Christmas . . .
    Bright liqueur, maple sap,
throat's lacquer, misnomer,
    namesake – couldn't quench
a thirst, of course,
    but gives occasion for it.

2. Lametta

Fuck me, I love that stuff —
    tinsel stripped
like a tarragon stalk
    of its million radial tines,
nervy with static
    in shredded cascades,
angle-confounding
    and biddable as a fistful
of grasshoppers.
    It implicates itself perpetually
in socks, hell-bent
    as Japanese knotweed
on travel, and infiltrates
    the kitchenette, which seems,
beside its disco stooks,
    too much of a muchness,
too matter-of-fact.
    Could we dress all utilities
in spangles of lametta,
    revel in the vulgar
Italian TV
    indestructible attention-splatter,
the cat-bewitching
    twitch and dangle, the dross?
Would things be worse
    or better?

3. Periptero

Apparently
      peripatetic, it pops up
wherever I go, glistening
      on my shoulder: gold epaulette,
albatross, piñata stuffed
      with bubble-gum, filter tips,
lottery tickets, mute
      cascades of laminated sleaze
difficult to care about,
      much harder to reject.
Less explicably there are
      sewing patterns, puzzle books
and tiny plastic helicopters
      bearing stigmata
from the moulds where they were cast.
      The proprietor slams
the shutters up
      and locks himself inside
like a djinn in a lamp,
      a night-busy, helping-hand
kobold in a kitchen,
      utterly invested in the enterprise,
inseparable from it. What
      is the epicentre everyone reports
but the staple through
      the nipple of a centrefold?

Caribou

With muzzles made blue
by the blue saxifrage they cultivate a weakness for,
their heart-shaped chests, their little bibs
and dewlaps fringed with long white hairs like radish roots,
they show how thin our myths for them are.

Photographed with people they look like props,
apologetically small and feminine;
but homogeneous in their landscape they make boulders shrink
and nature fits them to her fabric
of snow-melt and sedge most ingeniously. There is
something rabbity about them –

their soft splayed hooves and sensitive ears,
that give-away impractical tussock of a tail, spotless or mucky,
signalling over plains
or flashing downwards when they climb
rocky outcrops in waves with a sound like knuckles cracking.

Overburdened by antlers that spread like reasonable hands,
all palm, all paddle, they spoon the cold air
or with one jerk rip holes in clouds
the snow crowds through, corridors wolves can follow.

Sometimes in spring they swim five miles
and make the river crossing. Sometimes they drown
and their bodies bump downstream with the antlers interlocking:
young ones rub like fuzzy-felts,
old ones knock together with a warm woody thunk
like a wind-chime thinking.

They pass their grazing grounds, they pass the wood-chipping plants
and the hydroelectric, and a sleepy logger in a quilted shirt
feeding denuded logs down a flume.
Wherever they are going, those resinous eyes, resolutely unsoulful,
don't blink or flinch. They never change at all.

Octagonal Rug

Had the lion and the lamb lain down together, tannin lain down
with milk of lime, or Tannin lain with Metatron, the bronze and the grise,
the brown and the white, this flea-bag octagonal rug was the site.
Had the lion and the lamb thrown down their crests, the argent and the or,
the rampant charge and the muted shield, this was the field
of the cloth of gold, this was the league of corn. Here is a Tannenbaum
wreath in the snow. Here is a crown on a bandaged head.
This is at once the game and the ground. The lion and the lamb lie down.

The Eclipse

When it was time, we trooped outside – my brother, me,
my parents – through the open gates, and got clear of the trees
among crocuses and solemn strangers who gave sidelong
looks at the sky, as if it were the end of days and they expected
black riders or a plague of bees approaching.
Patchy cows languished in the next-but-one field.
Whatever you do, don't look directly at it, my mother said,
in a tone that never changed, whatever age the child.

You'll go blind, said my brother. Nobody corrected him.
Other people had made pinhole cameras out of cereal boxes.
You turned your back, and held the folded cardboard up
so the sun shone over your shoulder, like a teacher checking sums,
projecting itself in a golden cone on to the screen
where watching it change size posed no danger to your senses.
With a shudder, I thought, *What's there to stop
me looking at the sun? Nothing – only my resolve in between –*

then someone said, *Here we go!* As if my shudder had escaped
a shadow began to slide across the county. It looked like a wind
blowing candles out – the candles of white houses,
the candles of green trees, all bright points in uniformity dimmed
and left behind as the leading edge pressed on,
offering no resistance. That stone sliding shut across the face
of the sun shut the landscape too. It was all a projection.
My mother used to show us the blood dammed in her vein

by smoothing a fingertip across the back of her hand.
Into that same still fascinated time I passed when the skirt
of the shadow caught me up, leaching the warmth
from my scalp and face, as if I had been buried in morning sand.
What was dim already disappeared.
I stood at the lightless centre of the worst I'd always feared
before the finger lifted and the force of the heart,
reasserting itself, shot burnt umber back into the earth.

The sun's defeat made it seem less matriarchal
so I looked. Brightness caught me in the face so hard
my eyes flinched shut – but the sun in my head
remained: not yellow, not small,
not even exactly there, but definitely present, round but not a circle
and not so much bright or shiny as intense, meltingly intense,
a softness in the sky, an inwardness, where common sense failed,
like loose water seen through a weakness in the ice.

Memory Foam

A reek of paint
escaping from the vacuum-sealed
mattress puts me back
on a picnic table, overseeing
handymen creosote the fence,
with childish insistence
on being seen, on soppy adults
taking my impression
as the fat of my calves
took a rubbing of the table's grain
like a gravestone
copied with paper and crayon.

My colouring-in required
the same enormous concentration
each one of them devoted
to dipping wet stripes
from his prised-open tin
panel after panel;
trellises criss-crossed
like the undersoles of Converse
consolidated
at one sticky node, to which I pressed
my thumb when they'd gone,
registering something.

Habit comes
and takes my hand,
desire lines dear as the paths
across a palm,
each time I enter woodland
where the poachers advanced
and battle re-enactments
in civilian dress
laid the bracken
flat in the form of a beast
unrecognised yet:
here she sleeps.

Be it pines
rasping at cross-purposes
in the Trossachs
or sessile oaks in Ecclesall,
where the cross-pieces intersect
they chafe a bit
for want of humectant,
milling a fine
dust that all but disappears
under the ratcheting
shadow of the rendezvous
where it was born

or flares up bronze
if a footstep's pressure coincides
with the sun
as childhood can, caught
in a crossfire of sunbeams
as I am, embedded
here in the summer afternoon's
pallet of visco-
elastic polyurethane foam,
both firm and forgiving
of the body's form
and all its former trespasses.

The Historical Voice

The historical voice speaks when the fire's done burning
at a distance that is far but not inconceivably far from here.
In its vowels the Atlas bear and the tiger go on living.
The handful of things it tells us have been said before

and will be again, but it knows you're not the only person
left who failed to listen. Difficult words like *shame,*
fatigue and *dishonour* take shelter in its lexicon.
Nothing is dull but shines in its notice. It can fold time,

bringing two apparently unconnected matters together
in combinations meant to reconfigure your sense of scale:
a pin and the Pinwheel galaxy, a black hole and a feather.
It has no discoverable loyalties. Neither male nor female,

foreign or known, its accents come from anywhere
but here. The syntax it likes is clean, perhaps translated.
Rats and horses often appear, but metaphor is rarer
than the similes it finds to be more true, and underrated.

Knowing the worst, it speaks from that shadow. *We,*
it says, including itself, *we are like this. What has occurred*
cannot be hidden, perhaps not understood. It tends to be
more kindly than severe, less grave than good-humoured,

as if in exhausted agreement that we all now comprehend
the long half-life of cruelty – that love alone, however
prone it seems, can like a tiger worm live on sand.
It talks like this of love without incurring your disfavour.

A Shrunken Head

In the cargo hold,
cruising at thirty thousand feet
above blue islands,
galactically cold,
I float between Oxford and the site
where I was found

then traded on.
I cannot see for bubble-wrap.
At this stage
in my repatriation
I belong to no one, a blip,
a birdy ounce in the undercarriage.

Only the curator knows I've gone
and who is left.
She redesigns the tour:
lizard bones
replace me, indigenous crafts
distract with dyed feathers

from an absence. So
in me no memory withstood
the leather-thonged, moth-kissed
costume of an Eskimo,
its upright hood
ringed with reindeer fur like frost

regarding me for years
without a face
across the Victorian cabinets;
or a cruel long spear
frozen in space,
dressed like a wrist with jade and jet;

or Bobo — as I named him —
his heavy puss
pursed like a clown's,
like a freshly-sprung mushroom
observing silence . . .
I miss being part of the known

quantifiable index,
the massive mouths of children
smearing the glass case —
sometimes shocked
and crying, more often
delighted to learn of my fate,

sneaking pictures
for school reports. Their flashes
filled me up with light
like water
would a calabash
or cauterizing beams from night-

security did the displays.
For hours after
I'd see patterns that couldn't be real,
shadow plays,
huge birds fighting each other
up the loaded walls;

I'd imagine
hands to rub my eyelids with,
lift them and feel
the cross-stitches holding me in,
my vengeful breath
trapped beneath their seals,

wanting for the first
time in lifetimes to exhale,
to spit red berries
or the prattle of a curse . . .
then that would fail
in the force of my several injuries

and I'd seem to drop
towards a far ocean,
armless, footless, a seed-head blown
without will or hope
or wishing-upon
through the middle of a crown

to land on my shelf
under rows of wooden masks
and blown birds' eggs,
smelling the open jar of myself —
salt-sweet as tamarisk,
mild as figs.

Story

Under what tree, in what part of the forest, beside which branch
of the leaf-obstructed stream, in sun or in rain,

concreted into what foundation, supporting whose house, deaf
to how many dinner parties, subjected to how many holding-forths,

compacted along with what model of car, with what registration,
wearing which perfume and what sort of pearls,

in the back-of-beyond of what country, adjoining whose under-
development land, masked by which strain of animal fodder's

pollen blown from the next field along, belonging to whom, missed
by whom, questioned by which particular method, scarred where,

repaired where, reopened how, broken how,
how *taken care of*, transported how, buried

how, in what manner and from what platform disclaimed
during which international crisis, during which electoral year,

under whose watch, under whose watch
and why will it surface, why will it then be permitted to surface,

the end of the story, the body we need?

Acknowledgements

Poems from this book were first published in *Dear World & Everyone In It, Edinburgh Review,* the *Guardian, London Review of Books, Manchester Review, Modern Poetry in Translation,* the *Nation, Oxford Poets 2013, Poetry, Poetry London, Silk Road Review* and the *Times Literary Supplement,* and broadcast on BBC Radio 3 and Radio 4. 'Woodland Burial' was commissioned by the National Gallery for *Metamorphosis: Titian 2012.* My thanks to Arts Council England and the Authors' Foundation for their support. And thanks to Paul Batchelor most of all.